M000190157

≈175 Ways≈
To Advance
Your Career

By Don Kennedy

SuccessBooks
Atlanta, Georgia

Copyright © 1996 by Don Kennedy

Retail distribution by Longstreet Press
Marietta, Georgia

Cover by Deb Allread

Kennedy, Don -
        175 Ways To Advance Your Career.

        1. Career Development 2. Employees - Training of
        I. Title

ISBN 0-9640380-6-4

Printed in the United States of America
                    Printing 10 9 8 7 6 5 4 3 2

∽175 Ways∽
To Advance
Your Career

≈1≈
Identify what you are good at and enjoy.

Pick one area or field that would enable
you to utilize those strengths and
interests.

Over time, become excellent at it.

Demonstrate initiative.
Do tasks without being asked.

Perform every task, no matter how small,
the very best you can.

Look for ways to expand your job.
Do more than the description requires.

Do "whatever it takes" to get a job done.

8
Work harder than anyone else.

9
Be able to work as part of a team to
accomplish the company's goals.

≈10≈
Produce results.

Always be upbeat and enthusiastic, an
enjoyable person to be around.

Never do anything that might call
your integrity into question.

≈13≈
Be at work every day.

≈14≈
Get there early. Be willing to stay late.

≈15≋

Go the extra mile. Exceed people's
expectations every chance you get.

≈16≋

Set short-term and long-term
career goals.

≈17≋

Write them down and carry them with
you where you'll see them often.

18

Create a step-by-step plan for
achieving your goals.

19

Commit to reaching them
no matter what.

≈20≈

Don't confuse "activity" with "accomplishment." Do what's important.

≈21≈

Make decisions quickly based on the best information you have at the time.

22

Know your company's mission and let it guide your daily activities.

23

If your company has a budget, do your part in helping meet it.

24

Cooperate with other departments
in the company.

25

Volunteer to help with extra projects.

≈26≈

Don't habitually whine or complain.
If you have a problem with
something or someone, fix it.

∞27∞
Carry yourself confidently.

∞28∞
Speak confidently.

≈29≈
Look for ways to save the
company time and money.

≈30≈
Treat the company's money
like your own.

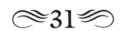

31
Answer your phone promptly.

32
Return calls promptly.

≈33≈

Don't drink on the job or
before going to work.

≈34≈

Don't do drugs at all.

35

When you speak, get to the point.

36

Don't talk too loudly, too softly,
or all the time.

≈37≈

Do the best you can in the job you have
right now even if it's not the one
you ultimately want.

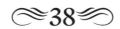

Make your boss look good, and try to
help advance his or her career.

Offer to assume tasks he or she
dislikes doing.

40

Actively network and build
"who you know."

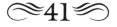

41

Develop long-term relationships
with those people.

≈42≈

Don't make a comment to an employee
of the opposite sex that you wouldn't
make in front of your mother or spouse.

≈43≈

Be cautious about becoming involved
in a work-related relationship.

≋44≋
Accept and learn from criticism.

≋45≋
Expand your vocabulary.

46

Fight for things you believe in,
but pick your battles carefully.

47

If you must confront a boss,
do it privately.

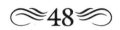

48

Get along with your boss. You're unlikely to get promoted, no matter how hard you work, if he or she doesn't like you.

Dress and maintain a hair style consistent
with your company's image.

Practice good basic personal hygiene.

⤳51⤳
Avoid bragging about how much
you make.

⤳52⤳
Avoid complaining about how much
you don't.

Page or call your boss at home
only if necessary.

Be prepared for the consequences if you
break chain of command and
go above his or her head.

≈55≈

Return early or on time from breaks.

≈56≈

Take one only when necessary
and only if everyone else does.

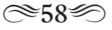

57

When someone is speaking to you,
give him or her your undivided
attention.

58

Listen more than you talk.

≈59≈
Write neatly, with no spelling errors,
and use correct grammar.

≈60≈
If you don't already know how to type
and use a computer – learn!

≈61≈
Know what your boss expects of you,
then demand an even higher
standard for yourself.

≈62≈
Be willing to travel if necessary.

≈63≈
Be willing to work weekends if necessary.

Build a record of tangible
accomplishments for which you
were directly responsible.

Tactfully make sure the right people
are aware of them.

Anticipate problems that could occur
and take steps to prevent them.

Immediately solve problems that do
occur before they become worse.

68

Believe there is a solution to every problem.

69

Ask for others input in solving problems.

≈70≈

Believe in yourself. Don't create imaginary limitations about how far you can rise or what you can achieve.

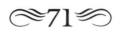

71

Listen to educational and
motivational audio tapes.

72

Attend educational and
motivational seminars.

73

Learn how to read others body
language, and be careful to
control your own.

74

Remember that how you say something
usually carries more weight
than what you say.

≈75≈

Take advantage of any optional training
programs offered by your company.

≈76≈

Take an outside executive development
or management course if your company
doesn't offer one.

≈77≈

Get as much formal education as is
necessary to reach your goals.

≈78≈

Remember that while "book sense" is
important, you must show
common sense, too.

≈79≈

Believe that people are basically good
and trustworthy (but keep your eyes
open and watch your back).

80

Teach others your job so the
company can promote you.

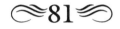

81

If you're skipped over for a promotion,
find out why and take corrective action.

Learn everything you can about your
company, not just the job you do for it.

Demonstrate unquestionable loyalty to
the company and to your boss.

Maintain a sense of balance between your career and the other important areas of your life.

Exercise regularly to maintain a high energy level and healthy appearance.

86

Read the trade magazines of your industry.

87

Attend conferences, conventions, and trade shows for it.

88

Never get complacent or think you know
it all. Keep learning, training, and
improving your skills.

89

Expect change.

90

Be flexible. It's okay to change the
direction to meet your goals, just not
your decision to get there.

∞91∞

Be willing to admit when
you've made a mistake.

∞92∞

Learn from it, and don't
make the same one twice.

93

Follow instructions.

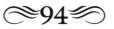

94

Follow rules and regulations.

≈95≈

Keep your personal problems from
affecting your professional performance.

≈96≈

Don't participate in office gossip.

97

Keep your promises.

98

Control your temper.

99

Don't wait for an annual review to know
how you're doing. Talk with your boss
throughout the year.

100

Do the same high level of work after a
review as you did before it.

≈101≈
Be willing to start at the bottom, get experience, and work your way up.

≈102≈

Respect authority.

≈103≈

Respect seniority, but realize it's usually
not the oldest employee in the
company who's at the top.

≈104≈

When calling on the phone or meeting someone in person, identify yourself before beginning a conversation.

≈105≈

Have a firm handshake.

≈106≈
Look people in the eye when speaking to them.

≈107≈
Remember their name, and call them by it when speaking to them.

Realize that your "people" skills can have
more to do with whether you advance
than your "technical" skills –
the best engineer or accountant
doesn't necessarily make a good
supervisor of other ones.

≈109≋

Be dependable.

≈110≋

Be assertive, but without being
pushy or rude.

≈111≈

Ask permission before
borrowing something.

≈112≈

When you do borrow something,
put it back where you found it.

113

Get tasks done as quickly and efficiently as possible.

114

Realize that "chit-chatting" in your neighbor's office doesn't count as work.

≈115≈
Work from a "To Do" list for each day.

≈116≈
Schedule time just for planning
and thinking.

≈117≈
Seek out job positions that will expose you to the most facets of your company and industry.

≈118≈
Seek out, talk with, and learn from others who have excelled in the field.

≈119≈

If your work has become boring, discuss with your boss how you could make it challenging again.

≈120≈

If you've achieved some success already, keep your ego in check.

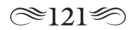
121

Consider changing jobs very carefully.
Don't drift aimlessly from
one to another.

≈122≈

Determine who is on the fast track in your company and try to develop a mentor-protege relationship with them.

≈123≈

Find out by what path the people already at the top of your company got there.

≈124≈
Allow time for delays in getting to
appointments, meetings, and airports.

≈125≈
Make use of waiting time by always
having work or a book with you.

≈126≈
Be positive. Expect and look for the
best in every situation.

≈127≈
Associate with other positive,
goal-oriented people.

≋128≋
Be creative. Look for ways to
stand out and be unique.

≋129≋
Know when it's smarter to
just go along and fit in.

≈130≈

Don't wait around and hope the right
things are going to happen for you.
Be proactive. Make them happen.

≈131≈
Accept that some things that
happen may be unfair.

≈132≈
Remember, however, it's not what
happens, but how you respond to it,
that counts.

≈133≈
Share the credit with others when
things go right.

≈134≈
Don't look for others to blame when
things go wrong.

 135

Do favors for people when moral,
reasonable, and possible.

 136

Praise others whenever possible.

≈137≈

Understand the numbers of your business that determine how well you and the company are doing.

≈138≈

Care how the company is doing, not just whether you get a paycheck from it.

≈139≈

Be respectful of how things have been
done in the past, but look for ways they
could be done better in the future.

≈140≈

If something is generally accepted as
impossible, prove that it isn't.

≈141≈

Know why something is being done
a certain way before trying
to change or improve it.

≈142≈

Evaluate how much time you spend
on the phone and what you
accomplish with it.

≈143≈

Make personal phone calls – particularly
long distance ones – on your time,
not the company's.

≈144≈
Be patient.

≈145≈
Ask for help when you need it.

≈146≈

Have good manners.

≈147≈

Have a great sense of humor.

≈148≈
Never bluff your employer about a better
job offer – you might be told to take it.

≈149≈

Stay alert for positions in your company that might be available soon.

≈150≈

Know which of your peers are your competition for those positions.

≈151≈

Make sure your boss is aware you want
more responsibility and the
opportunity to advance.

≈152≈

Take a promotion in title even if there
isn't an accompanying increase in salary.

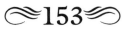

≈153≈
Become *the* authority in an area
vital to your company.

≈154≈

If your company has a newsletter,
contribute to it.

≈155≈

Speak to trade or professional
organizations as a representative
of the company.

156

Offer suggestions and ideas for
new products and services.

157

Whenever you're asked to do something,
don't always come back with an
alternative suggestion or idea.

Be careful about discussing company
business around strangers.

Don't criticize your company to people
outside of it – what you say just
might get back inside.

≈160≈

Respect all people regardless of gender, race, religion, or present job level.

≈161≈

Expect equal treatment regardless of your gender, race, or religion, but not special treatment because of it.

≈162≈
Check yourself out in a mirror during the day and brush your hair, fix your makeup, straighten your tie, etc. as needed.

≈163≈

Time carefully when you approach
your boss with an issue or request.

≈164≈

Participate in company-sponsored
civic, social, and charitable activities.

≈165≈

Join and become active in business and professional organizations in the field.

≈166≈

Become a confident public speaker by volunteering often or taking a course.

≈167≈
Don't maliciously use or "step on"
others in your quest for advancement.

≈168≈
Don't abuse your company's health plan
or sick leave policy.

≈169≈

Keep alert for events, trends, regulations,
or innovations that could negatively
impact your industry.

≈170≈

Look for events, trends, regulations, or
innovations you could take advantage of.

≈171≈
Be self-disciplined. Take the daily actions
necessary to reach your goals.

≈172≈
Continuously evaluate your progress and
make adjustments to stay on plan.

≈173≈
Take (calculated) risks.

≈174≈
Bounce back from all setbacks.

≈175≈
Never give up.

Show friends, employees, and customers you care with the advice that you share!

If you enjoyed the advice in this book, so will others. It makes the perfect • Employee or customer thank you • Meeting handout • Graduation gift • Incentive to purchase a certain $ amount or by a certain time • New employee welcome gift • Fundraiser • Christmas gift.

Ask your retailer about additional copies, or if unavailable, order with this offer and get one of our handy Pocket Reminders (see next page) FREE!

Corporate customizing and quantity discounts are also available for orders of 100 or more. Ask your ad specialty sales representative for details. Or, if you have received this copy as a gift, you may contact us at the address on the last page.

Use It or Lose It!

Only by seeing information repeatedly does a person remember it and use it.

So we put the top ten tips from this book on a durable plastic card that fits perfectly in any wallet or purse.

Use one to keep yourself on track or use them to train, motivate, or thank your employees or customers. There's a minimum order of three. But if you place an order now using this offer, we'll include another one for you – FREE!

(actual size $2^1/_4$" x $3^3/_8$")

How To Advance Your Career

1. Demonstrate initiative. Do tasks without being asked.
2. Perform every task - no matter how small - the very best you can.
3. Expand your job. Do more than the description requires.
4. Get the job done - produce results
5. Work well with others to accomplish the organization's goals.

Corporate customizing and quantity discounts available for orders of 250 or more. Ask your ad specialty sales representative for details. Or, if you received this book as a gift, you may contact us at the address on the last page.

Name _____ Title _____

Company _____

Address _____

City _____ State _____ Zipcode _____

Please call me about customization and quantity discounts. ( ) _____

Qty.	Item	Each	Total
_____	**175 Ways To Advance Your Career**	$5.95	_____
_____	Pocket Reminders (minimum quantity 3)	$1.95	_____
_____	*Bonus Pocket Reminder for ordering now!*	$0.00	FREE

- U.S. funds only

- Sorry, no CODs

- Make payable to SuccessBooks

Book=1/3 lb.; PR=1/16 lb.	
If weight	**Add**
0-1 lbs.	$3.00
1-10 lbs.	5.00
16-20 lbs.	7.00
Over 20 lbs.	+.50/lb.

Subtotal _____

←—— Processing & Postage _____
GA residents add 6% sales tax
(Law requires tax on shipping also)

Order Total _____

☐ Check ☐ Money Order ☐ MC/Visa/Amex _____

Signature (required) _____ Exp. Date_____

Dear Reader:

If you have helpful advice on how a business can better manage and motivate its employees, increase its sales, or improve its customer service, please jot it down and send it to us. We'll share it with readers in our upcoming books on those subjects and include your name in those books' acknowledgments.

SuccessBooks
6025 Sandy Springs Circle, Suite 350-BP
Atlanta, Georgia 30328-3863
(770) 410-0217